Porcupines

Lola M. Schaefer

Heinemann Library

Chicago, Illinois

Customer Service 888-454-2279
Visit our website at www.heinemannlibrary.com

Designed by Sue Emerson, Heinemann Library; Page layout by Que-Net Media
Printed and bound in the United States by Lake Book Manufacturing, Inc.
Photo research by Scott Braut

08 07 06 05 04
10 9 8 7 6 5 4 3 2 1

Library of Congress Cataloging-in-Publication Data
Schaefer, Lola M., 1950-
    Porcupines / Lola M. Schaefer.
        v. cm. – (Tiny-spiny animals)
Contents: What are porcupines? – Where do porcupines live? – What do porcupines look like? – What do porcupines feel like? – How do porcupines use their quills? – How big are porcupines? – How do porcupines move? – What do porcupines eat? – Where do new porcupines come from?
    ISBN 1-4034-3244-9 (HC), ISBN 1-4034-3329-1 (Pbk.)
    1. Porcupines–Juvenile literature. [1. Porcupines.] I. Title.
    QL737.R6S27 2003
    599.35'97–dc21

2003002073

Acknowledgments
The author and publishers are grateful to the following for permission to reproduce copyright material:
Title page Digital Vision/Getty Images; p. 4 Marian Bacon/Animals Animals; p. 5 Dan Suzio/Animals Animals; p. 6 Joe McDonald/Bruce Coleman Inc.; p. 7 Erwin and Peggy Bauer/Bruce Coleman Inc.; pp. 8, 16, 22, 24 Joe McDonald/Animals Animals; p. 9 Joe McDonald/Visuals Unlimited; p. 10 Donna Ikenberry/Animals Animals; p. 11 Laura Riley/Bruce Coleman Inc.; p. 12 P. Dotson/Photo Researchers, Inc.; p. 13 D. Cavagnaro/Visuals Unlimited; p. 14 Jim Schulz/Brookfield Zoo; pp. 15, 21 Tom & Pat Leeson/Photo Researchers, Inc.; p. 17 Steven Kraseman/DRK Photo; p. 18 Cosmo Blank/Photo Researchers, Inc.; p. 19 E&P Bauer/Bruce Coleman Inc.; p. 20 Laura Riley/Bruce Coleman Inc.; p. 23 (row 1, L-R) Donna Ikenberry/Animals Animals, Corbis, Heinemann Library; (row 2, L-R) Leonard Lee Rue III/Animals Animals, Corbis, Robert Lifson/Heinemann Library; (row 3, L-R) Corbis, Laura Riley/Bruce Coleman Inc., Ken Lucas/Visuals Unlimited; back cover (L-R) Leonard Lee Rue III/Animals Animals, Donna Ikenberry/Animals Animals

Cover photograph by Joe McDonald/Visuals Unlimited

Every effort has been made to contact copyright holders of any material reproduced in this book. Any omissions will be rectified in subsequent printings if notice is given to the publisher.

Special thanks to our advisory panel for their help in the preparation of this book:
Alice Bethke, Library Consultant
Palo Alto, CA

Eileen Day, Preschool Teacher
Chicago, IL

Kathleen Gilbert,
Second Grade Teacher
Round Rock, TX

Sandra Gilbert,
Library Media Specialist
Fiest Elementary School
Houston, TX

Jan Gobeille, Kindergarten Teacher
Garfield Elementary
Oakland, CA

Angela Leeper,
Educational Consultant
Wake Forest, NC

Some words are shown in bold, **like this.**
You can find them in the picture glossary on page 23.

Contents

What Are Porcupines?. 4

Where Do Porcupines Live? 6

What Do Porcupines Look Like?. 8

What Do Porcupines Feel Like?. 10

How Do Porcupines Use
    Their Quills?. 12

How Big Are Porcupines?. 14

How Do Porcupines Move?. 16

What Do Porcupines Eat? 18

Where Do New Porcupines
    Come From? 20

Quiz. 22

Picture Glossary 23

Note to Parents and Teachers. 24

Answers to Quiz. 24

Index 24

What Are Porcupines?

Porcupines are animals with bones.

They are **vertebrates**.

quills

Porcupines have long, round bodies.

They have sharp **quills** on their bodies and tails.

Where Do Porcupines Live?

Most porcupines live in the **forest**.

They eat and sleep in trees.

Some porcupines live in **deserts.**

Others live near rivers.

What Do Porcupines Look Like?

quills

claws

Porcupines look like hairy balls with **quills**.

They have sharp **claws** on each foot.

Porcupines' hair can be brown or black.

Their quills can be light brown or white.

What Do Porcupines Feel Like?

Porcupines' **quills** feel prickly.

The ends of their quills have sharp **barbs**.

But porcupines' hair is not prickly.

It is long and thick.

How Do Porcupines Use Their Quills?

Porcupines use the sharp **quills** on their tails to stay safe.

They shake their tails back and forth.

quills

Then, they hit their enemies with their quilled tails.

The sharp quills stick to their enemies.

How Big Are Porcupines?

Adult porcupines are as long as a person's arm.

They weigh as much as a large **pumpkin**.

Young porcupines are as long
as a **ruler**.

They weigh the same as a loaf
of bread.

How Do Porcupines Move?

Porcupines walk, but not fast or far.

They climb up and down trees.

Porcupines move around at night.

They are also good swimmers.

What Do Porcupines Eat?

Porcupines eat bark and branches.

They also eat leaves and flowers.

Some porcupines eat fruit and nuts.

This one is eating a berry.

Where Do New Porcupines Come From?

Female porcupines give birth to live babies.

These babies are called **porcupettes**.

Porcupettes drink their mothers' milk.

Soon they can walk with their mothers.

Quiz

What are these porcupine parts?

Can you find them in the book?

Look for answers on page 24.

Picture Glossary

barb
page 10

forest
page 6

quill
pages 5, 8, 9,
10, 12, 13

claw
page 8

porcupette
pages 20, 21

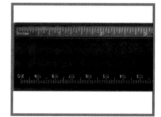

ruler
page 15

desert
page 7

pumpkin
page 14

vertebrate
(VUR-tuh-brate)
page 4

Note to Parents and Teachers

Reading for information is an important part of a child's literacy development. Learning begins with a question about something. Help children think of themselves as investigators and researchers by encouraging their questions about the world around them. Each chapter in this book begins with a question. Read the question together. Look at the pictures. Talk about what you think the answer might be. Then read the text to find out if your predictions were correct. Think of other questions you could ask about the topic, and discuss where you might find the answers.

! CAUTION: Remind children that it is not a good idea to handle wild animals. Children should wash their hands with soap and water after they touch any animal.

Index

baby 20
barb 10
bark 18
bone 4
branch 18
claw 8
forest 6
fruit 19
leaf 18
milk 21
nut 19
porcupette 20, 21

quill . . . 5, 8, 9, 10, 12, 13
river 7
tail 5, 12, 13
tree 6, 16
vertebrate 4

Answers to quiz on page 22

claws

quills